THE ADVENTURES OF MAX AND NED

Written by Mary K. Hawley
Illustrated by Rod McRae

CelebrationPress

An Imprint of ScottForesman

It was a dark and stormy night.

A long brown bus sped through the rain, packed full with the members of the Barnyard Big Band. After many months on tour, the band was headed for home.

Everyone was happy except for Max, the donkey. "I can't wait to be back in my own stall!" a horse said.

"I can," said Max. "Who wants to spend another boring winter on the farm?"

Suddenly there was a loud BANG. The bus tipped dangerously to one side.

"Oh, rats," said the bus driver, hanging on tightly to the wheel. "We have a flat tire." He brought the bus slowly to a stop. "It'll take me a while to change it," he said. "You might as well stay inside."

Max sighed. He looked out the window into the dark rain. Off in the distance, he noticed a tiny white light floating above the ground. "What's that?" he wondered.

Whooo—oooooo! A loud whistle filled the air.

3

The driver rushed back onto the bus. "There's a train coming!" he shouted. "Get off the bus, everybody! We're stuck on the tracks!"

The chickens clucked. The ducks quacked. The cows mooed so loudly everyone told them to hush. But all of the animals climbed off the bus as fast as their legs could take them.

The train raced toward the long brown bus. The animals and the driver watched nervously from a safe distance. With sparks flying, smoke rolling, and a loud clanging and hissing, the train came to a halt just a few inches from the bus.

"Hooray!" cried all the animals.

HOME
1234

"Why are you blocking the tracks?" yelled the train engineer.

"Sorry," said the bus driver, "we have a flat tire."

"Well, let me help you," said the engineer.

Just then the rain stopped.

As the moon came out from behind the clouds, the Barnyard animals stared at the passengers on the train.

"Wow, *wild* animals!" one of the chickens cackled to Max. "I thought they were only on TV."

HOME
1234

The other animals stepped down from the train. The lion spoke first.

"We are the members of the Sunshine Circus," he said politely. "And who might you be?"

"We're the Barnyard Big Band," answered a pig. "Pleased to meet you."

"Aaah, so you are also in show business," said the lion, licking his teeth. "I always like to meet other performers."

All the animals began to chatter at once. A nice-looking zebra came up to Max. "You're a donkey, aren't you?" he said. "I've read about donkeys. My name is Ned."

"I'm Max," said Max. "I never thought I'd meet a real zebra!"

"Where are you traveling?" asked Ned.

"We're on our way home to the farm," answered Max. "But if it were up to me, I'd go someplace exciting during the winter! Like—well, the place where *you* live."

"Our circus is also going home for the winter," said Ned. "If you can call a huge, wild savanna a *home*. We zebras are always running fifty miles this way for water, or thirty miles that way for a few dry mouthfuls of grass. And we're always watching out for lions. Even the one from the circus isn't very friendly."

"You live on a savanna? How wonderful!" Max said dreamily.

"Not to me!" said Ned. "I would love the quiet life of your barnyard, surrounded by cute little chickens and ducks. Tell me this, do they really let you sleep inside?"

"In the house?" Max exclaimed. "Oh, no! We're in the barn, of course."

"Oh, that's what I mean!" Ned sighed happily. "You sleep in a real barn! I suppose there are cows and things like that in your barn?"

"Oh, yes," said Max. "Cows and horses and sheep and pigs and everything. It gets awfully crowded."

"How lovely!" said Ned.

"Not really," said Max.

"I'd give anything . . . ," said Ned and Max at exactly the same time. They stared at each other. Their eyes glowed red in the moonlight.

"Are you thinking what I'm thinking?" asked Ned in an excited voice.

"How could we do it?" asked Max.

"I have an idea," Ned said, "but it has to be a secret. You know, our circus clowns have special makeup so maybe. . . ." Max's eyes widened as Ned whispered his plan.

14

Soon the bus had a spare tire in place.

A brown donkey climbed onto the bus. "Good-bye, Ned!" he called to a black and white zebra.

"Good-bye, Max!" answered the zebra. "Enjoy the farm!" The zebra trotted over to the train and climbed up the steps.

The bus driver honked the horn. The engineer blew the train whistle. Everyone waved for the last time.

The long brown bus moved on down the road and disappeared over a hill. The circus train chugged along the track, gathering speed as it headed into the sunrise.

16

On the train, a monkey sat down next to the zebra. "So Ned, what were you and that donkey talking about?" she asked. The zebra was silent.

"Ned?" said the monkey again. "Is something wrong?"

The zebra jumped. "Oh, you mean *me!*" he exclaimed. "And that donkey—you want to know what we talked about? Um, nothing, really!"

"Ned, go to sleep," the monkey said, shaking her head. "You don't sound like yourself."

A few hours later, the bus pulled into a large
farmyard.

"It's so *cute!*" the donkey squealed. "And
look—is that a pond? I mean—Look! The pond!
It's so *good* to see it again!"

The duck sitting next to the donkey looked at
him strangely. "Gee, Max, you've never cared about
the pond before. Are you feeling all right?"

"Oh, yes!" the donkey answered. "I've never
felt better."

Two months later, a letter for Mr. Max A. Donkey came to the barnyard. The donkey waited until everyone was taking a nap before he opened it.

February 15

Dear "Max,"

I'm having so much fun!

I love running with the herd for miles and miles, and sleeping outside at night under millions of stars. I've never felt so FREE!

Oops—have to run. I think I smell a lion.

Your friend,

the <u>real</u> Max

P. S. Vacation is almost over! The Sunshine Circus will arrive in New York on April 2nd. We'll stay at Mammal Towers, near Central Park. How about you?

Two weeks later, on a faraway savanna, a letter was dropped from an airplane.

"It's for you, Ned!" said the zebra who picked it up. The others were amazed. "Why, Ned! Open it! What does it say?"

But the zebra called "Ned" said, "Oh, I'm sure it's only junk mail." And he waited until he could sneak away to read it.

24